W9-CGY-108

PALOOKAVILLE

PALOOKA VILLE

SETH AND THE ART OF GRAPHIC AUTOBIOGRAPHY

TOM SMART

THE PORCUPINE'S QUILL

Library and Archives Canada Cataloguing in Publication

Smart, Tom, author
    Palookaville : Seth and the art of graphic autobiography
/ Tom Smart.

ISBN 978-0-88984-397-4 (paperback)

    1. Seth, 1962– — Criticism and interpretation. 2. Autobiographical
comic books, strips, etc. — History and criticism. 3. Autobiography in art.
I. Title.

PN6733.S48Z869 2016   741.5'971   C2016-905869-7

1   2   3   4   •   18   17   16

Published by The Porcupine's Quill, 68 Main Street, PO Box 160,
Erin, Ontario NOB 1TO. http://porcupinesquill.ca

Edited for the press by Chandra Wohleber.
Represented in Canada by Canadian Manda.
Trade orders are available from University of Toronto Press.

We acknowledge the support of the Ontario Arts Council and the
Canada Council for the Arts for our publishing program.
The financial support of the Ontario Media Development Corporation
and the Canada Book Fund is also gratefully acknowledged.

FOR SUSAN

CONTENTS

You can't fix yourself in time no matter how hard you try.
— Simon Matchcard, *Palookaville* #18

Seth, who lives in Guelph, Ontario, is an artist, author and cultural commentator, and one of the foremost graphic novelists working today. His unparalleled technical skills as a draughtsman and his unique ability to evoke an entire imaginative world based on a mythical mid-twentieth-century small Ontario town rank him as a gifted storyteller and part of a distinguished line of Canadian graphic designers.

But Seth can also be described as a sophisticated performance artist who cloaks his artistic practice in the garment of a cartoonist and illustrator. He is intent on examining the malleability of the comic book format to probe the nature and shape of time, and the many different ways that loss and longing can cloud one's memories of the past. His is an artistic practice that is entirely holistic. In his life he has immersed himself in the fashions, trappings, design motifs and manners of a mid-twentieth-century man. Just as the world he lives in echoes the past, so the world he describes in his art resonates with the same voice; this world has a fundamental integrity. Every detail is set down deliberately and with the intention of crafting an artistic reality that is true to what he sees as a period in Canada that existed perhaps a generation before he was born. His parents' time holds an uncanny allure for him, and he takes great pains to evoke it in the panels of his comic books, on the surfaces of his illustration boards and in the miniature buildings and streets that comprise his fictional southwestern Ontario town called Dominion.

Conjuring the past in sharp and distinctive lines: this is Seth's conceptual framework. His drawings are made with the purpose of being printed commercially in a number of formats — as single-panel comics, as multi-page comic books, book and magazine covers and as commercial or graphic illustrations for storybooks and novels. Drawings are made to serve the printing process. Graphic narrative is his expressive mode.

Beyond his signature style of clear outlines, easily identifiable figure types and evocative landscapes and scenes, Seth places great stock in the immersive possibilities of drawn and printed imagery to take an attentive reader back in time. He wants to draw us so completely into his art that a magical transformation is possible. The reader literally takes part in the story, falling into the time and place represented in the tales. To read a Seth comic is to enjoy an imaginative time trip that is unusually richly textured.

The trip, though, is not entirely the reader's. It is Seth's as well. By reading and looking closely at his work, and by knowing his proclivity for surrounding himself with mid-century fashion and design, we can see that there is a seamless link between outside and inside, and a very thin membrane between Seth's art and life. His art and life have many touch points; it is tempting to note that one reflects the other. His art depicts an imaginary dimension, and his life amplifies it. Conversely, the way in which he lives could be seen as providing inspiration for the material he sets down on his drawing paper. This close interaction between the lived and the drawn defines a unique dynamic: Seth performs his drawings as much as he makes them.

_____

PALOOKAVILLE

Let's take a close look at Seth's complex, dynamic art by studying his comic book series *Palookaville*. A close reading of this serialized book,

disguised as a graphic novel, reveals Seth's richly striated creative process and output. In its imaginative range, the scope of its themes, and even the wonderfully diverse ways the artist uses, manipulates and develops the cartoon and comic book formats, *Palookaville* is a remarkable testament to probing big, existential questions.

Its stylistic artistic antecedents are firmly in the graphic arts. Well versed in the history and development of the one-panel cartoon and the instalment-based comic book, Seth makes use of many of their forms, devices and conventions. He models his work, the flow of dialogue, set-up of a gag, pacing, composition of single panels and arrangement of panels on a page with art history in mind, particularly that of the cartoonists who worked in the magazine industry during its heyday in the middle of the twentieth century, drawing for weekly publications, among them *The New Yorker*. By absorbing the influences and examples of his elder peers, Seth acknowledges them, pays homage to them and makes wholly unique contributions to the art form from the foundation of the past. *Palookaville* stands on the shoulders of earlier generations of artists who developed serial comics, graphic novels and single-panel gags.

Beyond its artistic antecedents, *Palookaville* takes what came before and uses that to tell complicated narratives about life. Its overarching cadence is traced by the way Seth presents a complex thesis on the nature of life, on the elasticity of time, on the qualities of memory and on one's relationship to the past. He crafts these propositions in personal terms through the voices of his characters as they ruminate on their relationships to family and the community they live in.

Palookaville also presents highly entertaining stories of how times change due to economic vagaries beyond the control of any one person. Through the language with which Seth tells the stories of his complex characters, he sheds light on their pathos, and particularly on the hubris that makes them step away from the forces of change

and growth. In the relationships he describes among brothers and family members, he casts light on the sometimes idiosyncratic habits and behaviours that can and do disrupt lives. Above all, Seth masterfully takes his readers into the minds and psyches of his characters in fantastic ways; his portraits of depression, psychosis and even madness are gripping, real (perhaps true) descriptions of disturbing mental health conditions.

Palookaville does not tell only one story. It effectively uses the unique properties of the serialized format to impart several stories, each of which could be set down as a graphic novel in its own right. As of the writing of this book, Seth has produced twenty-two discrete issues of *Palookaville*. The first two relate stories about a gender-bending young man who is beaten up on the subway ('I Should'a Ran'). Another involves a coming-of-age romance in a Tilbury restaurant ('Beaches'), a graphic novella in two parts. Seth's more complex graphic novel 'It's a Good Life, If You Don't Weaken', takes up fully the next six issues as it tracks the search for a long-forgotten and obscure *New Yorker* cartoonist named Kalo. This is followed by 'Clyde Fans', an epic story in several parts, and now spanning twelve issues of *Palookaville*. Going back and forth in time, 'Clyde Fans' chronicles the rise and fall of a small industrial manufacturer and distributor as told through the relationship of brothers Abraham and Simon Matchcard.

Palookaville also throws into relief the nature of Seth's connection to the art he produces. In the series, Seth explores the depth of

16

the relationship of art to life, and whether it even matters if the art is a form of autobiographical storytelling. What is true is that Seth has produced an art of depth and nuance that speaks deeply about the passage of time and the capacity of art to shape it. In short, *Palookaville* is an audaciously original work of art. Its format as a comic book might mask the serious issues he probes through the art. But it doesn't.

WHO IS SETH?

'Seth' is the artistic doppelgänger of the man named Gregory Gallant, who was born in Clinton, Ontario, in 1962. A small town in the fertile, rolling hills of the Huron Tract on the windward side of Lake Huron, Clinton's roots are embedded in prosperous farming and forestry operations that have now passed. Gallant entered the world just as fortune was leaving Clinton. During the Second World War, its army base kept the local economy going, but the town fell on hard times in the late 1950s, particularly after the murder of a young Lynne Harper led to the wrongful conviction of Steven Truscott and the painting of the town as a notorious outpost of criminality. Today it is the home of Nobel Prize–winning author Alice Munro, who is Seth's favourite writer.[1]

We are never entirely sure if the Greg character in Seth's graphic novel *Nothing Lasts* is a fully formed self-portrait of the young Seth. However, the intimate manner in which Seth depicts the story's episodes convincingly leaves the impression that the older artist is

---

1 Seth writes this at the end of *Palookaville* #22 (Montreal: Drawn & Quarterly, April 2015). All issues of *Palookaville* are published by Drawn & Quarterly, and will hereafter be cited using the issue number and date of publication only.

telling truthful tales from his own past. *Nothing Lasts* is a sympathetic portrait of a boy realizing that he wants to be an artist, particularly a comic book artist. This detail runs parallel to Seth's own upbringing. In life, Seth drew his own densely illustrated comic books, populating them with superhero fantasy figures, an activity that he found satisfying for the way it let his imagination roam widely and that, at the same time, allowed him to develop his artistic talents in drawing and visual storytelling. These ingredients formed the foundation of *Palookaville.*

By the time Seth left high school he knew that he would be a cartoonist, and so he set off from Tilbury (where his parents had moved after leaving Clinton for nearby Bayfield and then Strathroy) to Toronto to attend the Ontario College of Art in 1980. His first published comics appeared in the Vortex Comics series *Mister X.* Following this he branched out into illustration work, which kept him going through the 1980s. In 1990, Seth began *Palooka-Ville.* It was one of the first to be published by the maverick Montreal house Drawn & Quarterly. Seth was lucky to end up at D&Q at a propitious time just as a so-called miniature boom in non-genre alternative comics was being felt in the industry and across the cultural landscape in Canada and the United States. Along with Seth, D&Q also published the semi-autobiographical work of his peers Chester Brown (b. 1960) and Joe Matt (b. 1963). The friendship of this young graphic novelist triumvirate even led them to include one another in their individual series.

'NOTHING LASTS'

What we can glean of young Gallant's life is (probably) described in 'Nothing Lasts', a series that was published in *Palookaville* #21 and #22.[2] In this (so far) two-part series, Seth sketches the outlines of a precocious boy who self-identifies as being on the edges of his society in small-town Ontario. Shy, picked on by bullies, more comfortable in a library than on a sports field, the young Seth/Greg is a misfit at school and left alone at home. As such, he finds comfort and escape in the comic books that are sold in the Big V drugstore next door to the library. Quickly learning when the new issues are due to arrive on the shelves, Greg makes it a highlight of his week to plot a shopping expedition to purchase his favourites. But he confesses that he is very shy about the whole endeavour; as Seth describes the shopping trips it is almost as if Greg were buying pornography rather than comic books. He takes great pains not to be seen by his schoolmates, furtively lurking in the store until the coast is clear and he can buy the issues without being 'caught'.

In addition to the theme of being outside the so-called embrace of his peers, Seth explores several others that serve to define the life of the strip's central character and which happen to have appeared in his earlier work. One is the relationship the character has to his mother as her marriage dissolves and his father disappears. Another revolves around the frequent childhood moves from one small town to another, from Clinton to Bayfield, Strathroy and then Tilbury. The

---

2 'Nothing Lasts', *Palookaville* #21 (September 2013); and *Palookaville* #22.

conflation of shyness, outsiderness and sexual confusion serves to colour the young boy's identity and view of the world. And yet another theme exposes the boy's inner world: his thoughts and fantasies and a proclivity to anger and aggression directed at his toys.

Even though 'Nothing Lasts' is a pseudo-autobiographical story of Greg's (Seth's) growing up and coming of age, it is told from the point of view of the adult Seth looking back on his past. As readers, we imbue the story with an element of trust. We believe that what Seth is telling us is true, and to the extent that it is, Seth the artist uses several literary and artistic devices to test the stories' veracity. On the one hand, the authorial voice narrates the episodes from the point of view of the present; he reminisces on past events; his memory is perceived as a reliable tool as he excavates the past. The style of drawing adds to the conceit of recalled personal history. The young protagonist is the central character who puzzles over the unknown events in his life that shaped his destiny and over which he had little or no control. For example, the moves from one place to another are put down as consequences of a father's inability to stay in one place. If there is a central trope to the autobiography, it is, paradoxically, unreliability. Greg is depicted as a willing, if powerless, agent in a picaresque story of movement, of marginalization and of being a loner who has few bearings or touchstones while groping toward self-definition as a

young adult. The narration takes the reader through episodes of finding and losing friends, of abandonment by an aloof father, of trying to preserve a relationship with his mother, of searching for creative fulfillment and of discovering his sexual identity.

IS THE NARRATOR RELIABLE?

The narrative voice tells the tales from two perspectives. Adult reminiscence is set down in an objective, first-person point of view. This is amplified by the characters' own dialogues and monologues told in the historical present tense. In the shift between the voices, Seth does manage to craft a patina of verisimilitude in the reader's mind. It is as if the adult author is saying, 'This and that actually happened, and to prove it, here is some dialogue from the times themselves.' The landscape too is a cozy theatre of small-town Ontario streets and lanes, which taken together reinforce the concept that the recalled history is accurate and fundamentally true.

But whether or not the portrait is true, all the reader can do is trust the author; if Seth says it happened just as he portrays it, then so be it. This reliability based on truth is where the dynamic action lies. In the overlap between history and memory, and in the apparent intersection between truthfulness and the clever use of literary device, Seth has crafted a potent creative landscape that allows all sorts of suspension of disbelief. In essence, accuracy really ceases to matter. By severing the fine line between fact and recollection, Seth liberates his autobiography from the constraints of historical veracity.

What he replaces it with is a captivating personal myth. His autobiography is shaped by the cadences of the picaresque narration. Here is the broad, heroic story that he tells in words and pictures: The young hero, born of a loving mother and distant father, is uprooted as a child and flung powerless into the embrace of a heartless, malevolent world in which he has only his wits and senses to find his bearings. His is a world of unusual banality, bereft of any cultural touchstones that could add meaning and depth to his experiences. In the absence of a cultivated atmosphere to breathe, the hero casts about in search of one in the landscape around him, and in the literature to which he exposes himself. In Greg's case it is the literature of the comic book involving emblems of heroic activity clothed in the costumes of the popular superhero.

Despite all the forces that he faces that could derail his pursuit of an identity as an artist — alienation, loss and longing, melancholy, bullying, self-doubt, shame, fear — Greg manages with some degree of success to find his latent voice as an artist — a cartoonist — and a means to allay the dragons (and bullies) that would keep him from his quest of self-definition.

To the degree that Seth has made the basic hero narrative conform to his own life story (or even self-selected his life stories to tell a heroic epic), he has successfully structured an autobiography. And he has convincingly told this mythic quest story (ostensibly *his* story) by moulding the conventions of romance to take place in the barren wastelands of the southwestern Ontario till plain in the 1960s. This is a very clever re-casting of the hero quest in the cartoon mode. Added to this narrative is the additional gloss that Seth provides in the way he conducts himself in real life. By adopting the fashions and by deliberately using a design vocabulary of mid-twentieth-century life, he emphatically points to this time and this persona as meaningful and truly reflecting his self-identity.

These themes, directions and iconographies all form the foundations of *Palookaville*. There is an electrical frisson in the work between the myth of Seth's life and the art that he uses to give it form, depth and texture. *Palookaville* is many things — comic, episodic story, fictional narratives, ironic commentary on form and function and a self-reflexive compendium of Seth's artistic sources and influences — but above all it is an entirely integral, fictional, artistic world that has its own reality. Of the many things it is and the stories it tells, it is clearly also a means of self-expression for Seth and a way to tell what we believe is a personal, life's story.

Let's now have a deeper look at *Palookaville* to discover how this is so.

WHAT AND WHERE IS PALOOKAVILLE?

The origins of the name 'Palookaville' rest in popular consciousness, particularly a movie starring Marlon Brando. It is the term used to describe the fictional place at the end of the line for a boxer who takes a dive in a fixed match, thus skewing the outcome to favour bets for his opponent, even if the opponent is clearly inferior. It is best remembered from a scene in Elia Kazan's classic 1954 film, *On the Waterfront*, which starred a young Brando as a washed-up boxer-turned-longshoreman-turned-informer named Terry Malloy.[3]

The film's most memorable scene takes place in the backseat of a

3   http://www.alternet.org/story/20776/ one-way_ticket_to_palookaville

taxi when Terry is talking to his disreputable brother, Charley, who threatens his brother with a gun not to testify against mobsters. During the encounter, Terry angrily reminds his brother that his earlier order to throw a fight had, in fact, ruined his boxing career, leaving him broken and bitter with not much more than 'a one-way ticket to Palookaville'. Nowadays, the term also has connotations of a large, clumsy man, an oaf, a bully or a brawler and is usually used in the phrase 'a big palooka!' The one-way ticket to Palookaville is a euphemism for being relegated to obscurity, to having been utterly defeated with almost no chance for redemption. Palookaville is the place at 'the end of the road'.

Seth has never been explicit about why he chose such a name for his comic book. What can be surmised from the stories that appear between its covers is that, in all of them, Seth takes great pains not only to describe and define characters, but also to provide a setting for the characters to live in and interact in. Place, it seems, has as much importance in *Palookaville* as does character. To a great degree, Seth's character-driven episodes take place in, are staged on, particular landscapes. And while these landscapes bear similarities to Seth's own home bases—Toronto's Cabbagetown; Bayfield; Tilbury; Strathroy; London—he draws them in dispiriting tones. They are impersonal, and at times even dangerous. They exist on the edges of someplace else. A big city looms at the limits of a neighbourhood or town; an avenue or alley lies off the beaten track; a dismal factory and apartment are in some nondescript corner of a place way out back of nowhere-land.

In general, the places that comprise Seth's comic book theatre are downcast, filled with melancholy, angst and anxiety. They seem to be shaded with the characters' own feelings of loss, alienation, hopelessness and despair at having missed out on opportunity because time has passed them by and left them to wonder at the nature and depths of their failures, if they even are given over to

thinking that deeply. In a very certain sense, Seth's characters seem to be stuck in the conditions they find themselves in. Trapped, unable to remove themselves from their paralytic circumstances and on a downward spiral, Seth's creations wander almost aimlessly from room to room, along grungy streets or through the urban decay looking for identities that they are destined never to find.

In short, as Seth portrays his existential Palookaville it is a soulless place of unrequited dreams and abandoned hope. Once there, it seems to a reader an almost impossible place to lift yourself out of. Arrival is a sentence imposed on the occupants by a malevolent force. You take a one-way ride there with little prospect of ever leaving.

Despite the heaviness of the place, Seth the artist approaches his descriptions of life in Palookaville with a light ironic touch that imbues his stories with humanity. His characters try to make the best of the virtues of their lot and somehow survive the soul-robbing vices that are its defining shadows. If Palookaville has place-specific references, they are cast in the light of the Brandoesque connotations of a place where losers live, where you are deposited after selling your soul and integrity. It is not populated by contenders or by somebodies. It is crowded with classless bums. Seth conscripted the name Palookaville as the edition's title.

POSSIBLE ORIGIN OF THE NAME 'SETH'

Why Seth? Despite the hint that his comic book would be autobiographically revealing, he does not give any definitive clues there as to why he chose the name. He remains mute on its origins even to this day. In several Western religions, Seth was the third son of Adam and Eve, and a substitute or replacement for the murdered Abel. In Egyptian mythology, Seth is an evil, canine-like, pointy-snouted god who murdered his brother Osiris and wounded his nephew Horus.

26

Another possible origin of the name may be in the work of an American author, poet, psychic and spirit medium named Jane Roberts (1929–1984). Over the course of her professional life, she claimed to have channelled a ghostly personality called Seth. While in a deep trance she is said to have allowed Seth to take control of her body and mind and to speak through her. Her transcriptions of tape recordings of Seth speaking through her earned her a pre-eminent place in the field of paranormal phenomena. Whatever its origins, the name Seth is freighted with a long and enigmatic etymology that now also embraces the artistic alter ego of Greg Gallant.

PALOOKAVILLE, FRONT TO BACK

All the above being said, there is an ingenious caginess in the writing, drawing and conception of *Palookaville* that Seth uses to full advantage. By appearing to mine the veins of autobiography, he deepens not only Greg's story, but also Seth's myth. Let's have a close look at *Palookaville* from its very beginning in 1991 to the present (issues #1 to #22) to see what is revealed about the author and about the myth.

The inaugural issue begins with a welcome by Seth. 'Yes, it's one of those one-name names (like Cher or Madonna),' he offers on the first page of his comic book with an added promise that 'personal details of my life' will be revealed in the coming issues.[4] Thus the complicated dance between art and life begins on the very first page of the very first issue. And the first instalment of the opening story seizes upon the genre-bending conceit; the character we first see in the drawn panels comes off as a comic book–style rendering of the type that over the years served to define the Greg/Seth character. In broad strokes, this persona is portrayed as a gentlemanly (almost courtly) figure, closely cropped, suave and a smoker. We quickly learn that this interlocutor was not always fashioned so; in an earlier life he had white hair because, he confesses, 'I was obsessed with having white hair. I really wanted people to mistake me for an albino.'

The first autobiographical episode unfolds even as the self-definition of the author takes on yet another colouring. Greg, Seth, croppy boy, albino: Seth the author delights in complicating his self-identity and enriching the comic/literary/artistic devices that serve autobiographical storytelling. Indeed, the first story features the troubles of the albino Mr Gallant, who is beaten by thugs who perceive him as gay. In this, Seth does not hold back on treating the theme of gay bashing in fairly graphic terms. 'They were beating me up for being gay,' Seth writes in the dialogue bubbles and in authorial commentary above them, 'and I let them think they were right!'

In the set-up for the first issue of *Palooka-Ville* (in later issues the title changes to *Palookaville*) and in its first panels, Seth deftly

---

4 *Palooka-Ville* #1 (April 1991), inside front cover. In the early issues of *Palookaville*, Seth varies both the spelling, first using a hyphenated version of the word, and the manner in which he indicates issue number by using the abbreviation 'No.' and the symbol '#'.

establishes what would be an overarching cadence in his artistic project, that it would be a kind of palimpsest. The so-called real person — the author and artist Greg Gallant — is at the centre of the skein of identities. Overlaid on this core is the persona of the gentlemanly Seth, an artistic avatar and manufactured identity taken on by Greg. In the telling of his stories, Greg mirrors his Seth-manufactured identity in the title character, who himself had a different self-identity as a manufactured albino. And, on top of all this, the prejudicial misreading of identity becomes the autobiographical episode's theme. The reader is cast into this tangled web of identities not entirely sure where truth lies, or whether it really matters. Whereas, in fact, it doesn't. Seth skilfully moves the narrative along, skating the line between what may be real and what appears to be real, letting readers find their own bearings in this clever hall of mirrors. In the episode's epilogue, Seth re-enters the story, perhaps to provide the reader with a moral exemplum. He relates that in the telling and retelling of the traumatic episode of the beating he is effective in building up a level of detachment from it. 'Over the years,' he offers, 'from retelling this story so many times it's lost a certain amount of reality for me.' Indeed, life retold as art establishes a kind of mythic lens that crystallizes the event and mitigates the traumatic pain.

In purely artistic and design terms, the first issue of *Palookaville* presents the story in a fairly straightforward fashion. The narrative structure, framed by a prologue and an epilogue, is that of a flashback told in the historical present tense. The comic book panels are direct, providing windows onto dialogue-driven narration with six panels on a page arranged in a grid format. As page design goes, it is a simple format that places emphasis on the drawn story, not on the elegance or complication of the overall layout. The comic's format follows the logic of a simple, sequential storyboard where the visuals serve the needs of the narration.

'BEACHES'

Palooka-Ville #2 builds on several of the foundational elements of the first issue, while also adding a self-reflexive conceit over the whole enterprise.[5] This is framed by the comic-book format itself and a Letters section that (to this author) seems to present letters received from actual readers commenting on the previous issue's contents, the artist, his style and influences as well as aesthetic touchstones. If this second issue has a subject, it is put down on the pages as two separate things: The story entitled 'Beaches'; and the epistolary commentary.

The story first. Just as the previous issue purports to be true to life, so too 'Beaches' lays down the conceit that it is anchored in a piece of Seth's late-adolescent life story. The grainy photograph on the inside cover (without commentary beyond the masthead information) deliberately, if lightly, glosses the graphic narrative that the reader is about to experience. In the same way that a W.G. Sebald novel also includes allusive, enigmatic grainy images to adumbrate the narrative, Seth appropriates the same device with a similar

---

5 *Palooka-Ville* #2 (September 1991).

Within the first panel: "Who knows what the original building looked like? By the late 70's, after a series of owners and poorly thought out additions, the Lighthouse Inn looked a hellofa lot like a refridgerater box, thrown on its's side, with windows punched out."

purpose, ostensibly to blur the line between fiction and fact, between life and myth, all the while freighting the drawn pictures with their own narrative line that runs parallel to, and may even intersect with the written words.

'Beaches' is the story of the protagonist Greg's summer of working at the Lighthouse Inn, a restaurant on Lake St. Clair at the mouth of the Thames River in southwestern Ontario. Seth designed his comic so that Greg could tell his story in the first person. The opening pages of the graphic novella narrate the banal details of a mundane summer job and the misfit cast of characters that make up Greg's co-workers. Although 'Beaches' opens with a retrospective narrative structure, Seth adds other storytelling devices that give a satisfying complexity to a simple recounting of romance and lost innocence. Panels with no voiceover commentary or even dialogue bubbles advance the action simply through drawing, mimicking a cinematic storyboard.

Palooka-Ville #3 contains the second part of 'Beaches', chronicling Greg's affair with a woman named Beaches, wife of the Lighthouse Inn's owner.[6] Just as in the first part, the second tells Greg's story of

6   *Palooka-Ville* #3 (June 1993).

love and disappointment with a touching sensitivity and a ring of authenticity. The narrative is also structured to circle back to the enigmatic first panels and explain the action that Seth has depicted. One compelling feature about this part of the story is Seth's depiction of a thought dream involving Greg in a boat that winds up getting swamped, and with Greg fearing that he is drowning. This episode also takes us back to an earlier, unexplained image: the cover of the issue, which depicts the penultimate moment in the story and in the dream — of the moment it begins to rain on the boat.

But we don't read any commentary on this work until *Palooka-Ville* #4, which has a Letters section and a Glossary printed on its inside front cover.[7] Of the previous issue's cover, David Tompkins of New York writes to Seth that, 'Your cover is mysteriously beautiful. There's something still, serene to it — the arrested moment, pregnant with the violence of the breaking storm. You've caught the first few dreamy seconds of cataclysm. A lovely job.'[8]

Above all, 'Beaches' shows Seth exploring the elasticity of the comic book format. The drawings are clearly delineated, balancing

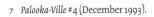

7 *Palooka-Ville* #4 (December 1993).

8 Ibid.

compositions involving single and multiple figures, context, close-up, overhead and straight-on points of view, and to a limited extent demonstrating how one panel can direct the eye to the next through dynamic lines, the contrast of light and dark or even the gazes of the characters described in the panels. The interplay of formal variety, characterization, delineation and dialogue with Seth's evidently wry, ironic eye makes for engaging reading. As you read the novella, it becomes increasingly clear that Seth has a keen eye for details, an ear for idiomatic phrasing and an empathic sensibility that makes 'Beaches' in its totality seem genuine.

'LETTERS' AND ARTISTIC CONTEXTS

The Letters section printed on the back cover at the conclusion of Part 1 of 'Beaches' inaugurated a feature of *Palookaville* that appears in nearly every subsequent issue. Additionally, along with the main story, Seth craftily emblazons the front and back pages with departments that range over the years from a 'Department Store' or related photographs, cartoons and other ephemera that augment the content of the stories. In the Letters section, frequently titled 'Dear Sir', there is an element of self-reference: the authorial commentary that often follows a letter is a kind of quizzical remark or a response to a query. Other information in the department sections takes the form of smaller-format bulletin advertisements that promote sales of Seth's drawings, panels, sketches and related material, or provide information as to his comings and goings. Dates of speaking engagements, travels, publication information or even just a tip-of-the-hat acknowledgement of gratitude to readers or hosts whose hospitality Seth has enjoyed while travelling.

Yet entwined in this diverse array of information, Seth salts in contextual clues about his influences and sources, ideas and motivations, and even a tipoff (through the notes from letter writers) as to his purposes in portraying certain plotlines and characters in previously published issues. While there is a tongue-in-cheek conceit that the letters were written by unique individuals, there is a strong sense when reading them (at least to me) that they may, in fact, have been penned by Seth himself, even though he claims otherwise.[9] Notwithstanding their authorial provenance, the letters provide valuable, pithy nuggets of information that illuminate the art historical contexts around the graphic art and even what simply interests the artist.

For example, in one of the first published letters, Mark Burbey from San Francisco (one of the many letter writers who signed his name and place of residence, but beyond these bare bones remains an anonymous, curious epistolarian) writes to Seth that he is, 'really taken with your style of drawing, and your coloring is just the coolest.… Your art is … witty and expressive and comforting and fun. There is a naturalness about it, a substantial lightness.… A perfect blend of contemporary illustration and magazine styles from the '30s and '40s, or so it seems to me.'[10] And so there is. In this very first letter, its writer introduces a theme to this department that, over several subsequent issues, introduces and discusses in epistolary fashion, Seth's artistic antecedents, stylistic touchstones and some of his favourite artists. As David Tompkins from New York observes in his letter, *Palooka-Ville's* 'low-key elegance puts one in mind say, of James Thurber.'[11]

It does, a fact emphasized by the prosaic doodle at the centre of the Letters page of a hapless Thurber-esque character stepping along

---

9   Email to author, January 6, 2016.

10 *Palooka-Ville* #2, Letters, inside back cover.

11 Ibid.

in a spaced-out trance. It is as if the opportunity of the letter format might well be giving Seth the chance and the licence to add disguised commentary on his own work, and in the process point to its aesthetic provenance in the context of mid-twentieth-century magazine illustration, cartooning and comic books.

Without doubt, in his approach to graphic style and, in certain respects, to the voice of his strip, Seth fell under the spell of James Thurber (1894–1961), one of the more influential cartoonists of his day. He came to fame for his work published in *The New Yorker* chronicling the outer and inner lives of Walter Mitty, a henpecked, set-upon misfit and his overbearing, demanding wife. Thurber gave Mitty a wicked and vivid imaginative life that provided him an escape from the drudgery and nagging of his unfortunate marital fate. Thurber's graphic style is linear and simple such that the images seem to appear aimlessly from doodled sketches; Seth emulated some of this to good effect in the characterizations in his early stories.

In addition to being a stylistic influence, Thurber's sharply ironic sensibility gave Seth a kind of authorial voice to mimic, particularly in passages that require first-person narration of thoughts by the drawn character, or editorial commentary on a scenario. Seth learned much from Thurber's example, especially how to describe in words and pictures the interior landscapes of motivation and emotion that drive action and storylines in the drawn panels. As Malcolm Bourne of Lancashire notes in his analytical letter to Seth, in words that could also be aptly applied to Thurber's style, 'I think the vital ingredient which made the difference was that you didn't go for a deliberately exaggerated illustration style or unnecessary crudity of expression. Your work was … stylised and stylish, but there was nothing to clog up the scenery and get in the way of the reader.'[12] Clarity of expression and

---

12 *Palooka-Ville* #2, Letters, inside back cover.

voice were given high marks by Bourne because, as he writes, 'I could simply take in the story, absorb it, and find enough to think about, without using a metaphorical machete to hack through any superimposed layering.'

Just as Seth's letter-writing fans noted his affinity to the earlier generation, some also pointed to his contemporary comic- and cartoon-drawing peers, all of whom were being published by Drawn & Quarterly. Pittsburgh's Randy Costanza was full of praise for this young Canadian cohort whose output, he infers in his letter, ranked with the best of the American cartoonists. 'You Canadians are great,' he intones in his letter. 'People like you, Chester Brown, Julie Doucet, and Joe Matt are like the Crumbs, Hernandezs [*sic*], Clowes and Bagges [*sic*] of Canada.'[13]

High praise, indeed. Also, it is a-none-too-subtle ranking of the D&Q Rat Pack (which included Brown, Doucet, Matt and others) with the founders and mavericks of the underground comix movement of the past four decades.[14] The references, whether from real people or seemingly written for the department by the author himself, introduce a self-referential element of *Palooka-Ville*, and are an important source of information on the stylistic antecedents that influenced Seth's artistic production. Over the course of the next several issues of the comic, much is revealed about the comic's artistic genome in the letters, as well as in the glossary, and to some degree even in the serialized graphic novel 'It's a Good Life, If You Don't Weaken'. But more on that later on.

By pointing out the influence of Robert Crumb (b. 1943), Gilbert

---

13   *Palooka-Ville* #2, Letters, inside back cover.

14   For a history of Drawn & Quarterly, refer to Tom Devlin, editor, *Drawn and Quarterly: Twenty-five Years of Contemporary Cartooning, Comics, and Graphic Novels* (Montreal: Drawn & Quarterly, 2015).

Hernandez (b. 1957), Daniel Clowes (b. 1961) and Peter Bagge (b. 1957), Americans all, the work of Seth and his Canadian cohort was situated in the context of artists all working within the rich late-twentieth-century mainstream and countercultural comics/comix. This movement sprawls across the creative territory of mainstream contemporary comic art, its alternative underground subculture, and the historical past's inspired individualists and *enfants terrible*. Crumb, for example, has long been viewed as the master and eccentric rebel of the underground comic movement of the 1970s, as author and artist of *Zap Comix*, and creator of characters Fritz the Cat, Mr Natural and others. His work is characterized by its rebarbative voice and deliberately fashioned outsider status, but it also plays a close, cool line between fiction, fantasy, shock and autobiography. In the early years of the new century, the art-curatorial community embraced Crumb, with his work being included in important international exhibitions, including the Carnegie International.

YOUNG CONTEMPORARIES

Hernandez, Clowes and Bagge, half a generation younger than Crumb, have developed their reputations as comic artists by absorbing and re-defining several formats and conventions of comic book art and cartooning. Hernandez, aka Beto, created a type of magic-realist comic format that glanced off the styles and vocabularies of Marvel and DC Comics. His work endures for the manner in which he develops complex characters, particularly women. Clowes is recognized as one of the so-called Generation X cartoonists of the 1980s alternative comics scene, who played a central role in elevating the movement to a place where it received critical notice from reviewers and academics and gained a broad readership. His *Ghost World* was one of the first 'literary' comics that was sold in mainstream bookstores under the category of 'graphic novel'.[15] Clowes's work, like that of his peers Chris Ware (b. 1967) and Art Spiegelman (b. 1948), reflects its author's interest in referencing the history, drawing styles, layouts and colouring of earlier newspaper cartoon strips, especially those published in the Sunday papers of the mid-twentieth century. Clowes's work is bathed in a kind of retrospective homage to the form, while also redefining it by commenting on contemporary themes relevant to the lives of a new, hip young readership. And so too does Bagge's. But whereas Clowes quotes the visual vocabulary of the Sunday funnies, Bagge developed a static but elastic dynamic style that owes its debt to the 1940s cartoons of Warner Brothers' Bob Clampett (1913–1984).

A GLOSSARY

By the time Seth began drawing the fourth issue of *Palooka-Ville* his work was being tagged as laid back[16], classic[17], and marvellously evocative of the northern midwest.[18] Perhaps wanting to burnish further the aesthetic and historical contexts surrounding what he was doing and why, in *Palooka-Ville* #4 Seth established a glossary that runs on the same page as Letters. It lists comic book artists and cartoonists who exerted important influences on Seth, or whose styles Seth paid attention to. As it is published in each issue, the glossary adds contextual historical weight to the work while also framing the feature story itself. This touching, multi-part graphic novel recounting the protagonist's research on the art and life of Jack 'Kalo' Kalloway, is ostensibly

---

15   https://en.wikipedia.org/wiki/Daniel_Clowes

16   Adrian Tomine, Sacramento, CA., 'Letter' (*Palooka-Ville* #4).

17   Andy Hartzell, Las Vegas, NV., 'Letter' (*Palooka-Ville* #4).

18   Ibid.

also a search (perhaps the author's own) for and definition of the roots of his own artistic identity.

Seth's glossary of influences is catholic and eclectic, spanning a spectrum from the very well-known to the obscure and including specialists and curators of the subject. At the top of the list, Seth puts master cartoonist[19] Charles M. Schulz (1922–2000). Writing, 'I can't over-emphasize the effect this man's work has had on me,' Seth salutes the single most important influence on his personal style. It might seem odd that he points to the creator of *Peanuts* and its unforgettable characters Charlie Brown, Snoopy, Lucy, Linus et al. After all, *Peanuts* is the story of a gang of kids coming to terms with life's lessons in an adult-less world. On the surface, Seth emulates Schulz's clean, elegant line-drawing style. Like his artistic elder, Seth holds a high regard for clarity and stylistic precision, and for achieving a signature style and then not changing it. Seth was likely also drawn to the softly stated moral exemplums embedded in the storylines, often articulated by the child philosopher Linus. The world of *Peanuts* is an amber-encased *bijou* of a wisely innocent childhood in which the contrasting forces of good and evil can be seen in the interactions of children.

---

19 *Palooka-Ville* #4, Glossary, inside back cover.

But beyond style and moral tone, Seth was doubtlessly capti-
vated by the fact that Schulz created a strip that freezes time. Schulz's
characters never age; the episodes all take place in a time-capsule
world defined by the interactions of character only. The context in
which they 'live' is undefined and, in fact, not important, and they
appear to have no history beyond what takes place entirely in the
present tense. Schulz's world is an existential metaphor. The characters act and interact in a balm of timelessness. This element of
Schulz's work remains the most significant legacy that so inspired
Seth. The quest to fix things in time by stopping time became the
overriding arc in Seth's art and, to a great extent, in his life, right from
the earliest days of his professional practice.

In addition to Schulz, Seth's glossary contains the names of other
artists whose work affected him in one way or another. Ludwig
Bemelmans (1898–1962), author of the Madeline series and whose
work appeared on many a *New Yorker* cover over the years, makes the
list. Just as Schulz created a frozen time capsule, so too did Bemelmans in the storybook telling of the adventures and escapades of a
precocious Parisian schoolgirl, her eleven classmates at a convent
school and Miss Clavel, a nun who presides over her young charges.
Another of *The New Yorker's* prominent cartoonists, Whitney Darrow,
Jr. (1909–1999), is also listed in Seth's glossary because, as he notes,

Darrow's cartoons are 'very appealing to the eye'. The list goes on to include Dr Seuss (Theodor Seuss Geisel, 1904–1991), whom Seth calls 'the genius of children's books'. Other *New Yorker* cartoonists he cites are Peter Arno (1904–1968), whose work mocking the cultured urbanites of the day reflects, says Seth, 'pure modernity [in its] bold lines, masterful compositions'; Helen E. Hokinson (1893–1949); and Chas Addams ('king of the macabre', 1912–1988). Syndicated cartoonist Syd Hoff (1912–2004) and William Steig (1907–2003), among others, round out the first glossary.[20]

What is abundantly evident from this initial enumeration of sources is that Seth identified primarily with cartoonists whose reputation and fame rest on (1) the work they did in the so-called golden years of American magazine cartooning — the middle decades of the twentieth century and (2) cartoons that were published in *The New Yorker*. While the reasons he gives for his affection for these artists are pithy, in subsequent issues of *Palooka-Ville* he elaborates on the nature of their influence in words, and more interestingly, in the graphic styles he adopts in his own work.

'IT'S A GOOD LIFE, IF YOU DON'T WEAKEN'

The first story in *Palooka-Ville* #4 begins with a confession. Seth comes clean, writing that, '[cartoons] have always been a big part of my life. Ever since I was a very little kid they had a real strong effect on me.'[21] 'It's a Good Life, If You Don't Weaken' is a dispiriting story of the protagonist's (Seth's?) search for information and artwork by and about a

---

20 *Palooka-Ville* #4, Glossary, inside back cover.

21 'It's a Good Life, If You Don't Weaken', *Palooka-Ville* #4.

forgotten 1940s cartoonist pen-named Kalo. In essence, it is a search for an aesthetic ground zero for the contemporary cohort of young comic book artists and cartoonists. Convinced that their immediate predecessors lacked a rich and deep artistic tradition to offer them, seeing only superheroes, gag strips, and pornography, in their own work, Seth's artistic peers felt a need to look further back in time to find and define their intellectual and creative provenances.[22] 'It's a Good Life' charts one such search and the emotions that motivated it. In its spirit and latent message, Seth's graphic novel looks to the work of '50s *New Yorker* cartoonist Peter Arno and his contemporaries, who mocked their own society and that of typical readers of the magazine. Stylistically, Seth's drawings reflect these antecedents as well in his use of dynamic curved contour lines bordering areas of solid grey tonalities.

Although it's a doleful tale, Seth does tell it well and with a degree of visual and narrative assurance. Told from the first-person point of view, the opening panels of 'It's a Good Life' set up the tantalizing conceit that this is the author's personal story, an important episode in an autobiography. The unnamed main character is a version of the now

---

22 http://www.hipmuseum.com/good.html

familiar Sethian type—a man with closely cropped hair wearing a classic, wide-brimmed fedora and Burberry-style trench coat. The effect of the drawing and the narrative voice creates an intimate yet detached relationship between author and reader. The sense of intimacy is reinforced by the early confessional tone of the narrator, who admits that comics 'occupy a BIG part of my brain. It seems like I'm always relating things that happen to me back to some mouldy old comic gag or something like that.'[23] His life, it would appear, is shaped by comic book art. Life imitating art, the protagonist allows that, 'It's silly, but I swear, I can't do much of anything without—I mean, I can hardly tell someone I love them without dragging Dr Seuss, old Bemelmans or the inimitable Mr Schulz into it.'[24]

The central quest for Kalo's identity that fills 'It's a Good Life' is both the fictionalized research path our hero takes as well as a way for the real-life Seth to begin laying a sound methodological track for artistic sources and references for his own artistic practice. Thus, he includes in his story references to his creative heroes. Whitney Darrow figures prominently, particularly his sexist and raunchy pulp

---

23 'It's a Good Life, If You Don't Weaken', p. 1.

24 Ibid.

comic 'The Office Party',[25] which our story's hero picked up on an impulse. We are further told that this book began what would become 'a lifetime interest in the cartoons of the old *New Yorker*'.[26]

As the first part of 'It's a Good Life' moves along, a few of Seth's familiar tropes are exposed in the thoughts of the characters. The first-person narrative voice alternates between a retrospective point of view and a real-time chronology of events. We are introduced to the protagonist's family: his dull, unambitious brother and his mother (no father figure is present). There is also the concept of unchanging time; our hero complains that at his mother's home 'nothing changes ... well, none of the important things. No matter how many times I go away, when I come back it's the same. I count on it to stay that way ... I retreat to these memories often when I'm depressed.'[27]

If we were ever in doubt that 'It's a Good Life' is autobiographical, Seth either disabuses us of that doubt or confounds us even further in the story's second part, when the main character's sidekick,

---

25 Corey Ford, illustrated by Whitney Darrow, Jr., *The Office Party* (New York: Doubleday, 1951).

26 'It's a Good Life, If You Don't Weaken'; p. 1.

27 Ibid.

Chet, calls our hero by name: Seth.[28] This cartoon Seth is a worrier, an anxious young man who appears to have very little self-confidence. This tosses him into frequent spells of depression, a condition he puts down as a consequence of the fact that he is 'too goddam judgemental'. He also longs for the past as a vaguely utopian state of changeless grace. 'I do think life was simpler then,' he muses, '... easier for people to find personal happiness.'[29]

True or imagined, a palpable sense of loss fills the panels of 'It's a Good Life', while providing an emotional field for reading the quest plotline. Loss is not just framed in terms of the imagined ease of life in the past. Cartoon Seth bemoans the loss of craft and facility in the way things are drawn between past and present; he holds up the incongruous example of Kalo ('He kinda draws like you,' Chet observes)[30] as evidence of what he is preaching. Thus, the narrative action is set up and propelled by the agents of loss and resentment—that the present is an unrefined time and that quality draughtsmanship is no longer appreciated as it once was. In Seth's

---

28 'It's a Good Life, If You Don't Weaken'; p. 1.

29 Ibid.

30 Ibid.

mind, Kalo embodies a kind of artistic purity fixed in the amber of his very few extant cartoons. By delving into a search for this man's historical identity, Seth believes that he might possibly learn something truthful about himself, about something timeless that is buried in his own artistic genetic code. It is as if real-life Seth is saying through cartoon Seth that the results of the quest might well convey on him 'a good life' if they do not weaken him before he achieves the prize.

CHARACTERS WHO MAKE SETH SAD

Thus the story of 'It's a Good Life' is set up as Seth's (author and character) search to find out as much as he can about 'the pretty obscure' Kalo.[31] Picking up on the themes and structure of issue #4, *Palooka-Ville* #5 shows Seth as a ruminative artist deliberately blurring the lines between fiction and autobiography to such an extent that the distinction becomes irrelevant. And to a very great extent it does read as autobiography, largely due to the artist's clever development of the conceits he has set up in his comic book. The fictional story is about the search for artistic roots. The structural apparatus with which he frames the story—the Letters and the Glossary—amplify the cartoon story's theme by presenting the author's further enumeration of comic and cartoon artists that influenced his work.

The second part of the novel opens with a nearly cinematic, silent portrayal of Seth taking a late-night skate on a frozen pond. The action unfolds as would a film's storyline, with the authorial voice laid in as the omniscient first-person narrator. Seth places the reader in the privileged position of hearing the character's thoughts, particularly about how he balances his expectations with what turns

31 'It's a Good Life, If You Don't Weaken', Part Two, *Palooka-Ville* #5 (May 5, 1994).

out to be the truth — the theme of the issue and of the quest for Kalo's identity. 'It's funny y'know,' Seth muses, 'no matter what I talk about it inevitably leads back to cartooning,' an admission that to a great degree his life is given shape and texture through the gloss of cartooning. Our Seths see the stories of their lives cast as panels on a page. When read in sequence, the panels tell of expectations met or dashed.

As Seth skates he mines his influences and motivations for being a cartoonist, eventually pointing to another important influence that set him on his life's path: Jimmy Hatlo (1897–1963), cartoonist and author of the strips *They'll Do It Every Time* and *Little Iodine* ('the little girl character was the first image that stirred sexual feeling in me' as a six-year-old).[32] Hatlo's caricatural style and screwball comic gags gave Seth a period voice that found gentle absurdities in daily life. Seth also points out that, while he is influenced by many a cartoonist and comic book artist, he is 'definitely not aping anyone's style. I have been influenced by a wide variety of old cartoonists,' he admits, '… but I do certainly fall into the school of "little feet" artists (such as Irving Tripp, Sam Cobean, Hergé and Jack Markow).'[33] Stylistic

32 'It's a Good Life, If You Don't Weaken', Part Two, *Palooka-Ville* #5 (May 5, 1994).

33 'Dear Sir', *Palooka-Ville* #6 (November 1994), inside back cover.

references and search for influences aside, *Palooka-Ville* #5 gives us insights into Seth's deep interest in the past and his melancholy at not being able to capture and hold time still. Several passages that play out over sequences of panels are tellingly introspective. When cartoon Seth speaks, he might well be voicing the thoughts of his creator, real-life Seth. Take, for example:

If you don't like 'navel-gazers' you wouldn't much care for me. I'm immersed in my past — wallowing in it. I look at my childhood and it's like some golden key. If I just ponder it, sift through it, pick at it enough, I feel like I'll find the answer to every goddamn thing that's wrong with me now. Leave me alone for five minutes and I'm slipping into some kind of depression. It's just that everything makes me sad.[34]

Other nostalgic influences that he dredges up from his childhood and says have a kind of sad aura around them include a holy trinity of cartoon characters from the popular Sunday paper strips. He admits to loving them with a sad sort of love: Nancy, Andy Capp and Little Nipper. Why do these characters make Seth sad? Likely anticipating this question, Seth surmises that the melancholy they evoke may well be due to the fact that 'they were passed on to me by my parents'. From his mother he inherited an affection for Nancy and Andy Capp, and from his father his esteem for Little Nipper and the strip's author, Canadian cartoonist Doug Wright (1917–1983). Seth's affection for these strips is irrevocably tinged with feelings of loss. They also crystallized in him a conviction that he would 'be happier living in the past — the '20s and '30s specifically'.[35] Loss and longing were fuelled by his wish that the better elements of those decades had somehow

---

34 'It's a Good Life, If You Don't Weaken', Part Two, *Palooka-Ville* #5.

35 Ibid.

survived into his own lifetime. For Seth, the traces of that time that have managed to live into his present day are no more than remnants 'of some ghost world' that has long vanished, as have his parents.

With the second part of 'It's a Good Life' Seth has crafted a compelling graphic elegy, a complex, pliant lament for absent parents, a dirge for the distant passing of childhood, a requiem for the interwar period of the twentieth century. The search for Kalo, ostensibly the real story of 'It's a Good Life', is a metaphor of emotional excavation to discover the source of psychological unease and the roots of sadness. When challenged by his girlfriend in issue #6 that, 'You REALLY don't like things changing do you?', Seth answers truthfully, 'No … I guess not. When something is nice I like it to stay that way. … As awful as things are right now, I'd be more than happy if the world would just stay relatively like this until I die.'[36]

---

36 'It's a Good Life, If You Don't Weaken', Part Three, *Palooka-Ville* #6.

THE MAN CALLED KALO

Kalo is the nom-de-plume of a cartoonist who briefly contributed to *The New Yorker*, then retired in obscurity in small-town southwestern Ontario. When Seth sets out to research the man and the art he starts with the bare bones of a biography — that he was born in Goderich, Ontario, on May 13, 1914, and died on November 6, 1979, in Strathroy, just a few kilometres away from his birthplace.

Seth describes the search through a series of dynamic panels of travels from Union Station in Toronto through the southern Ontario countryside to the humble, tidy station in Strathroy. The sequences are conceived and drawn as if they were storyboards for a film. We easily give ourselves over to the cinematic sweep and cadences of the journey in search of an elusive quarry. We are treated to close-ups and overhead shots, profiles and cameos of specific urban sites and rural landscapes. Seth also reminds us that he sees his trek in terms of a comic book allusion — in this case to Hergé's (1907–1983) *Tintin* cartoons featured in the adventure story 'The Black Island'.

While loss is a primary theme in 'It's a Good Life,' by the third part of the story Seth broadens its range to explore the manner in which landscape and place prompt memories and associations, or

I think of Tintin when I see Inca relics and pendulums and plus-fours too ... but, of course, I see a lot more trains than any of those things.

what he calls 'good things',[37] in a personal quest. For Seth good things are moments of revelation when it appears as if time miraculously stands still and the past and present condense into a mystical eternal present. 'Here's what kills me,' Seth admits of his love of train travel, 'whenever I'm travelling around Ontario I'm really keeping my eyes open for them [good things]. Where I think I see them? I'm not even sure where they're located. I guess near Strathroy ... but maybe not. Maybe London. Or Grand Bend. They're probably long gone anyway. It's not like I'm expecting some grand epiphany or anything ... but it would be nice to wander into some town or turn a corner and find them there, still standing. That would be nice.'[38]

Kalo, then, is a complicated construction of identity, and the biographical hunt is framed as a mythic quest for the self. By searching for and finding out about Kalo's life and art, Seth hopes to discover truths about his own past and present, and to recover from an abidingly deep sense of loss. Perhaps Seth gives a clue as to his motivations for retrieving elements of the past through a cartoon strip and graphic novel by using (or publishing) words from one of his fans, a

------

37 'It's a Good Life, If You Don't Weaken', Part Three, *Palooka-Ville* #6.
38 Ibid.

Karen Hirsch of Brooklyn, who writes that, rather than being a voyage into depression and melancholy, mining the past as an artistic project has merit as a cathartic process. Of the Kalo search, she states:

Your work gets stronger and stronger. This latest is intricate and classy and quite moving. What touches me most are your passages about feeling immersed in the past, particularly your own. I feel quite the same way. But is it really depression in such meditative moments? For me, it's more of a wistfulness, or at worst, a melancholy. Depression is, to me, a fear of, and denial of life, a place where nothing is meaningful. What you seem to find in paint shop windows and on antique store shelves is just the opposite — an awareness of life: the histories of objects, and of the people who owned, made and loved them. The sadness comes, I suppose, from sensing how much is past and irrevocable. There are times when every little thing is poignant, when

you long for moments (people, places) even as you are experiencing them. Some lucky folk can banish this nostalgia, and simply *live*. They don't 'ponder it, sift through it, pick at it.' The wallowing and collecting is often, it seems, an attempt to stave off loss, to not forget.[39]

As *Palooka-Ville* #7 opens with Part 4 of 'It's a Good Life' the reader is taken on a visual trek along with Seth, researching Kalo, to Strathroy—a hunt that blends with a retreat into Seth's own past.[40] The opening panels are beautifully drawn to evoke the protagonist's trudge through the town and eventually to the house where he lived for five years during childhood. As cartoon Seth gazes at his boyhood home, recalling memories of living there, the narrative introduces a dream sequence of him as a child playing in the rain. Memories give way to an authorial voiceover musing on the past and on how the 1950s conjures up a sense of national identity in him. 'Somehow or other,' he realizes, 'the '50s always seem very Canadian to me. When I think of the States, I think of the '40s—but Canada—the '50s. Why is that? I guess it could be the CBC television I watched as a kid.... These associations—they govern so much of our thinking.'[41]

This particular *Palooka-Ville* issue stands out from the others in Seth's admission of several maxims of his personal philosophy as well—aphorisms that are expressed by cartoon characters. Seth comes clean that he, just as Linus (of *Peanuts* fame), prefers to avoid problems, so Seth confesses to himself and to the reader that, 'No problem is so big or complicated that it can't be run away from.'[42] This issue is also noteworthy for its long glossary on the issue's back

39 'Dear Sir', *Palooka-Ville* #6.

40 *Palooka-Ville* #7 (April 1995).

41 Ibid.

42 Ibid.

cover that provides a list of cartoonists who, in some manner, were important to Seth or who were mentioned in the graphic story. One artist on the list is Helen E. Hokinson, a *New Yorker* cartoonist known for her breezy cartoon strips and magazine covers about the New York modern woman of the 1920s and '30s, particularly a stuffy type of privileged uptown matron.

Another artist who finds himself in Seth's glossary for this issue is H. T. Webster (1885–1952), an ironist among whose strips are the well-known, syndicated *Life's Darkest Moment*, *The Timid Soul*, *How to Torture Your Husband* and *How to Torture Your Wife*, all of which comprise witty, succinct jabs at people and circumstances that take on an oversized aura of self-importance. His art is characterized by well-drawn depictions of stuffed shirts, milquetoasts and inflated egos brought down to earth by precisely directed barbs issued from the cartoonist's penetrating gaze. Webster's reputation rests to a large extent on the manner in which he was able to capture a psychology of timidity in which the kind and gentle soul was bulldozed by the unintended slights and ignorant meanness that are part of everyday life.

A Canadian cartoonist, Jimmy Frise (1891–1948), also made Seth's list. Frise's densely populated and expertly drawn strip *Birdseye Center* was a regular feature of the *Toronto Daily Star* from the 1920s to the '40s. By poking gentle fun at Upper Canada society, particularly the

rural towns of central Ontario, it served as an escape from the modern age by lampooning the fast-disappearing farm kids who were transplanted into the growing metropolis.

Other artists highlighted in subsequent iterations of his glossary are British Columbia–born gag cartoonist Robert Jefferson (Jeff) Keate (1912–1995) — Seth calls his a 'simple but ugly style. Strangely appealing though.' Another artist is Henry Boltinoff (1914–2001) — 'his work appeared just about everywhere from the '30s on to the '60s' — a humour and comic book artist, and editor for DC comics.[43] Also listed is Robert Kraus (1925–2001) — 'Not a real favourite of mine but he's amusing every so often' — a regular *New Yorker* contributor of cartoons and covers, and later a children's book author and illustrator.[44]

If there is a common theme in the work of the artists populating Seth's glossary, it lies in the intersection between humour and commentary. He reaches for cartoonists who have an identifiable personal

43 'Dear Sir', *Palooka-Ville* #8 (December 1995), inside back cover.

44 'Dear Sir', *Palooka-Ville* #9 (June 1996), inside front cover.

style that combines dynamic linearity with structure and compositional integrity. Hokinson's lyrical line describing her characters' gestures tells much about their emotions and sense of privilege; linear action and a focus on retributive justice in small, unguarded moments, Webster's gags aim to pop inflated self-important bombast while sketching a society of innocent bullying and self-deprecation; and Frise developed a visual language of nostalgia for a mythical time in Canadian society that likely never existed. The connecting line through the selection seems to be that these artists all developed iconographies that expose the hidden biases of privilege as seen from the point of view of a percipient, shrewd author/cartoonist.

Seth absorbed much from those populating his glossary, not the least being the quality of perspicacity. His characters, particularly Seth, combine shrewd observation with intuition, self-awareness with a tincture of neuroses, and wisdom with street smarts. Seth the artist subordinates part of his strip to a personal philosophy mouthed by his drawn avatars. *Palooka-Ville* #8, for example, recounts a conversation between Seth and his chum Chet, in which our brooding protagonist ruminates on decay and loss in a way that (it is attractive to think) exactly echoes the author's own thoughts. Their dialogue revolves around Seth's opinion that 'things are obviously getting worse every year' and that people are in some manner or another 'fucked up' by some sort of trauma.[45] But beyond the emotional baggage that is loaded onto Seth's quest for Kalo, the style of the strips themselves defines a rare form of visual poetry. Alternating between first- and third-person points of view gives the reader a privileged, if detached, vantage on the scene; Seth draws events as they happen to the protagonist all the while recording an interior monologue. Text and picture provide parallel narratives that intersect at some points and diverge at others. A David Garland of Brooklyn sums this quality up best in his letter: 'I love that it shows you doing one thing while the verbal narrative is on a different topic, and then we see you telling your friend about the activity, but not the thoughts...'[46]

At its heart, 'It's a Good Life' is an elegy and a lament for the inevitable march of time and the reduction of all things to ashes that fade in the fog of memory. Seth has expertly wrapped up these two types of loss in the metaphor of a search for an obscure, undistinguished cartoonist. In a strange way, by interpreting the quest in the form of a pseudo-autobiographical graphic novel, Seth elevates what might otherwise be a dull personality to a higher, ennobled status as an autonomous human being with a family and a personal if mundane history. He points to an earlier time, a generation or two in the past, as simpler and perhaps even nobler than is generally assumed. Not just a story filled with pathos, 'It's a Good Life' is a many-layered exemplum on mortality, fate and in many respects, the meaning of life.

If 'It's a Good Life' has a moral, it appears in *Palooka-Ville* #9, which contains the graphic novel's last part. Seth asks Kalo's best friend, Ken Tremblay, about Kalo's life and art, and whether it mattered to him that he 'let go of the cartooning.' Ken ducks describing Kalo's philosophy, but responds with his own: 'When you get to be

---

45   'Dear Sir', *Palooka-Ville* #8.

46   'Dear Sir', *Palooka-Ville* #9.

my age you discover that everything mattered. Life isn't a series of good and bad choices. It's harder to steer it one way or the other than most people think. You just get pulled along. You look back and you wonder 'could I have changed the course of my life?' Maybe you could've … but it would probably have taken a tremendous force of will.'[47] Being pulled along by events, by the vagaries of time and circumstance: as long as you willingly give yourself over to this fate, Seth seems to be telling his readers, it's a good life if you do not weaken. But, in truth, you have weakened.

'CLYDE FANS'

'Clyde Fans', a multi-part graphic novel whose first instalment was published in *Palooka-Ville* #10, is a story about two brothers, Abraham (Abe) and Simon Matchcard,[48] told in alternating scenes from the past and present. It is a story of loss, regret and melancholy. Picking up on that of 'It's a Good Life', the moral of 'Clyde Fans' is expressed

---

47 'Dear Sir', *Palooka-Ville* #9.

48 'Clyde Fans', *Palooka-Ville* #10 (April 1997).

early on by Abe: 'It's funny how long a man can simply keep doing what he's always done — no matter how futile. Day in, day out … while the world goes on without noticing.'[49] Fatalistic inevitability, persistence and their corrosive effects are Seth's grand themes in this darkly beautiful, complicated and complex graphic novel.

In it Seth demonstrates the range of his visual and verbal storytelling skills. Originally published in 1997, the first pages of its panels take the reader inside the offices and apartments that comprise the Clyde Fans Company. In fact, as we come to learn in retrospect, the interior of this building — its rooms and corridors, closets, and basement furnace room and storage areas — is a key character in the brothers' stories. As Abe walks through the building he relates his cardinal rules of making a successful sales pitch, a diatribe that takes the story back nearly half a century to 1949 and the days of travelling salesmen. As the narrative unfolds, the lesson that emerges for the reader is how unremarkable Abe's life really is, despite his amplifying its importance in his monologue. The narrative, it seems, is propelled as much by Abe's pacing through rooms as by Seth's use of the walking conceit as a natural storytelling device. Perambulation,

---

49 'Clyde Fans, Part One, continued', *Palooka-Ville* #11 (October 1997).

used as a narrative trope, often figures prominently in 'Clyde Fans'.

The paradoxical structure of the tale is established as a foundational element early on — Abe's self-importance is in stark contrast to the banality of his job as a fan manufacturer and distributor in the years leading up to the invention of the air conditioner. Building on this innate bifurcated narrative reality, we are introduced to Abe's brother, Simon, a timid milquetoast figure, who evidently suffers from anxiety and other neuroses and psychoses. As strong, forceful and self-determined as Abe appears to be, Simon is the opposite: a mild-mannered soul with little or no self-confidence, who finds himself in the unenviable position of working with and for his brother as the family business starts to fail. Suffering from what seems like agoraphobia, Simon would rather stay home reading and attending to his collection of fool-the-eye photographic postcards that use drastically disconnected juxtapositions to give a sense of spectacularly unreal realities. Of the few truths that Abe utters over the course of the novel, none is more prescient than his characterization of his brother: 'Now if I had to envision a vocation for Simon,' he states in the opening panels of Part 1, 'I think something like prisoner would be more in line.'[50]

---

50 'Clyde Fans', *Palooka-Ville* #10.

As passionate as Abe is for gadgets—radio and television—Simon is for reading. Abe is a man of action, Simon is a man who enjoys the passive, contemplative life of the mind and arts. Simon is ruminative, doubting, always self-questioning, and so too is Abe, but in a different way. Where Simon knows he is not suited to the life of a travelling salesman, Abe is slow to realize late in his life that some of the choices he made in the past—some of his inactions—ultimately led to his ruin and the failure of his business. 'I was genuinely surprised by the speed in which I was left behind,' he admits as an old, lonely man who pathetically points to a batch of purchase orders as the only proof that 'I once existed.'[51]

PROOF OF A LIFE LIVED

What constitutes proof of a life lived? A job, a title, a successful life, a family? In both brothers' worlds there is a common vacuum at their centres. Neither has made much of his destiny beyond a litany of failures. If anything, 'Clyde Fans' is a tragedy—a forlorn tale of two

---

51 Ibid.

unimpressive people on whom fate appears to have played a malicious trick, leaving them ruined and alone. As Seth describes his characters pictorially there is an odd symmetry in the apparent paradox of their self definitions. Although they appear to be opposite sides of the coin, they are, in fact, Gemini twins representing eternally duelling aspects of the same soul, cartoon yin-yang complements rattling around in a busted-up building, itself a metaphor of the human heart. This sense is described in a letter by Robin Koustabaris, from Vancouver, published at the end of Part 1. Robin writes:

When I sit down and read PV, usually after a few minutes reality drains away and I am sucked into the quiet, contemplative rhythms of the drawings, panel after silent panel, and I can almost hear the drawing thinking. It is the reading experience that is closest to a walk in the woods that I have found. You somehow manage to draw history into each form, and even when they depict something modern-style they still carry the weight of the past, as if the shapes contain all the manifestations of themselves that came before them…. It's in time, yet somehow out of time.[52]

This summarizes a direction that Seth takes in this story. His purpose

------

52 'Dear Sir', *Palooka-Ville* #10.

is to compress past and present to show how decisions made in years gone by have an impact on the present, and how revisiting the past presents a temptation to editorialize or even romanticize a reliable sequence of events and the motivations for actions. As we follow Abe as he meanders around, we feel a palpable heartbreaking anxiety as we come to terms with the fact that Abe's self-justification is just so much hot air blown from the mouth of a self-deluded narrator.

Unquestionably, Seth found his voice and mode in the 'Clyde Fans' drawings and story. His crisply delineated panels are sure and clear, as is the fictional world he depicts precisely in the circumscribed building's interior. 'Nothing's keeping me here,' Abe brags of his so-called home and office. 'I could leave anytime I wanted. Unlike Simon, I never saw this place as a cage.'[53] But he never did leave and while it may not be his 'cage', the interior has an oppressive Kafkaesque weirdness. This is made all the stranger by the authorial point of view — the interior monologue places the reader inside Abe's head where we get front-row access to a small, self-important view of things pronounced with the authority of a potentate. The question remains: Is Abe speaking to the reader, or merely justifying to himself

---

53 'Clyde Fans, Part One, continued', *Palooka-Ville* #11.

all the misguided decisions he has made over his life and business career? Is he seeking proof of a life well lived, or just proving he lived?

LOSS AND THE PASSAGE OF TIME

True to the familiar over-arching theme that Seth tracks to great effect in his work, 'Clyde Fans' is a pictorial disquisition on the passage of time. Abe shelters his deep-seated fear of change in the comforts of routine, which he confesses he embraced while his brother gave in to it. Indeed, the profundity of Seth's 'Clyde Fans' lies in the way he layers the closed, claustrophobic corridors of the musty office and apartment with feelings of hopelessness, despair, anxiety and self-delusion by creating complex characters who are in deep denial that their lives are object lessons in failure—failure to adapt, grow, learn and change in smart ways. Abe and Simon exhibit a shocking inability to see the future unfold and a baleful disability to apply intuition to solve the challenges they face.

This is a potent scenario for any author, let alone Seth. The tragic arc of loss propels the narrative momentum of 'Clyde Fans'. It captures readers, hurling them along through the episodes, parts and volumes of *Palooka-Ville*. Given the blurred lines that Seth so effec-

tively draws between fiction and autobiography, the reader might continually wonder if he is using the microphone of the graphic novel to probe from many different viewpoints the meaning of *tempus fugit*. Certainly there is an inbred tautology in the clever blurring. The words his characters speak ultimately come from *his* mouth and pen.

To read Seth, and in particular 'Clyde Fans', is to be led along a winding path that touches on big existential questions posed from the points of view of two lonely brothers who ran a small manufacturing company into the ground. Just as Canute seeks to hold back the tides, Abe and Simon stubbornly try to avoid any sort of change as a way to confront the frightening need to adapt. 'You know, when you get older, you don't change. Don't let anyone tell you that you do,' Abe avers in one of his more fatalistic moments of self-justification. 'Don't let anyone tell you that you do. You stay the same. If anything, you become even more entrenched in the patterns of behaviour you've always shown.'[54] The narrative voice is almost casual, loquacious, as Abe wanders from room to room, stopping briefly to ruminate on something, pee, take a bath, fix dinner and then continue on.

The heaviness of Abe's depressing homily is framed by Seth's

---

54 'Clyde Fans, Part One, continued', *Palooka-Ville* #11.

panels that show him comfortable in exploring not just the expressive dimensions of a single frame, but also the integrated interaction of panels working together on a page and across a double-page spread. Take, for example, his illustrations showing Abe walking down the basement stairs and into the furnace room (*Palooka-Ville* #11, pages 28–29). The interaction and contrasts of light and dark on the page coupled with the direction of Abe's stroll betray a cartoonist in control of the formal elements of cartooning and exhibiting a high degree of confident draughtsmanship. There is an overall integrity to the page's composition where individual panels work together to direct the eye, adding emphasis and momentum to the narrative. Silent panels balance speaking ones; altogether there is a pleasing rhythm in the way the monologue unfolds. It reads as authentic. One can imagine this very sequence as being real. Formal and design contrasts are equally matched in the characters of the brothers. Abe and Simon are described as being as different as night and day. Simon is characterized in the language usually reserved to describe an artist. 'Really, he was very handy with a pen.' Abe admits about his brother, 'He spent a lot of time and effort designing … things.'[55]

---

55 'Clyde Fans, Part One, continued', *Palooka-Ville* #11.

THE NATURE OF REALITY

In addition to wrapping his mind around the substance and passage of time, Abe wonders about the nature of reality. In what is likely one of the more original ways in which this dissertation has been presented, Seth uses Abe's cogitations as a means to explore the nature of 'the real world'.[56] In this piece, Seth reveals his hand just a bit to point to the significance of the meaning of the apartment as a metaphor of reality. The interior of the apartment is a cleverly disguised representation of the interior of Abe's and Simon's whole world. As Abe puts it, 'The office existed as some sort of intermediary level between reality and this hidden place. In a way it's all backwards referring to the outside as reality. It's only in here that anything ever felt real. Out there everything was empty and hollow.'[57]

Thus, Abe (and Seth) comes clean about the world they both have created: Abe, his apartment and office refuge; and Seth, his graphic novel. The 'only in here' is revealing for both the fictional

---

56   Ibid.

57   Ibid.

character and the author himself. Where, both ask, does reality lie? In the context of a cartoon confession, the reality of the 'in here' has extra resonance to the extent that, if Abe is a Sethian doppelgänger, then fiction is a real place of self-actualization while 'out there' is a formless, empty, hollow realm of alienation and self-loathing. Art, Seth (through Abe) points out, is reality, a place where chaos has a form.

THE FRENCH-BELGIAN TRADITION

The 'Dear Sir' printed on the back cover of issue #11 contains further clues to Seth's stylistic antecedents and favourites in the comic book genre of the mid-twentieth century, but this time with a definite French-Belgian connection. Jean-Bernard Lauze of Montpellier, France, writes in his letter (in the pseudo-cryptic voice of archly trans- lated epistolary prose), that 'It's a Good Life' 'procured to me much enjoyment'.[58] He goes on to compare the graphic style to that of sev- eral French comic book artists and cartoonists, among them *Tintin* author, Hergé; Seth's clean line reminded the letter writer of the expressive and gestural clarity of a *Tintin* graphic novel. He also cites Yves Chaland, Serge Clerc, François Avril and Dupuy and Berbérian as artists to whom Seth's work bears an affinity.

Just what might such an affinity be? Chaland (1957–1990) is known for his crisply rendered retro 1950s style in which a dynamic linearity conveys action and adventure. His panels show a strong sense of structure and composition that span the two-page spreads in an overall, integral look. Clerc (b. 1957), on the other hand, drew his cartoons and illustrations in an angular, mannered style to convey a lusty sensuality that harkens back to a late 1950s and early 1960s

---

58 'Dear Sir', *Palooka-Ville* #11, inside back cover.

jet-age modernism. Avril's (b. 1961) work combines hard-edged contours with brushed washes in tones that give an effect of lightness and tropical summer heat. His is an evocative, moody interpretation of the 1950s, where the monuments of modernism dwarf humans — buildings, cities, abstract painting and what-have-you. Philippe Dupuy (b. 1960) and Charles Berbérian (b. 1959) are cartoonist collaborators whose collective reputation rests on their graphic narratives featuring the laconic single-man character Monsieur Jean. Theirs is a breezy storytelling mode that appears untutored, yet reflects a careful attention to structure, line and detail, as well as a form of comic-book truthfulness about the passage of the protagonist through early male adulthood.

The extent to which the work of these artists and their French and Belgian artistic contexts are pointed out in Lauze's letter may well be a clever way for Seth to direct critical eyes to the widening foundation of his own artistic lineage and interests. A reader, once again, is left with the vague feeling that the letters were written — ghostwritten — by the artist himself as a way to build a meta-narrative on top of the drawn pages. Whether or not they have a single author, the letters and their commentary provide important information about the artistic context in which Seth is working. In light of Lauze's observations, 'Clyde Fans' can be viewed and appreciated through an international gloss. Although a place- and time-specific story of a fictional, ordinary southern Ontario life of decline and loss, Seth's art resonates when placed next to that of his French and Belgian contemporaries who were developing their own traditions. As the French and Belgians were cinematic in their ambitions, so Seth also set down his stories in a manner that is nearly filmic; they pick up on the vocabulary of the close-up, the pan and the overhead shot, as well as using light and dark to emphasize mood and emotion. Beyond the obvious stylistic and narrative affinities between Seth and his French-Belgian brethren, Seth likely also channelled the latent

melancholy that can be discerned to greater or lesser extent in each of the artists enumerated by his letter-writing fan. Although approaching their individual art from different and divergent directions, each developed a unique narrative and pictorial language of loss, alienation, confusion and perplexity.

DREAMS AND SURREALISM

Just when you think you have Seth pinned down — an original Canadian voice blending a *New Yorker* cartoon joined with a love of Gallic composition and attitude — he turns in a new direction. With *Palookaville* #12 Seth explores the ways in which he could convey the strangeness of dreaming and the oddness of surreal juxtapositions in his panels, and wrap them in Abe's and Simon's stories.[59] He also teases the attentive reader with tantalizing clues implying that, in fact, there is a link between fictional Simon's story and his own life story.

Issue #12 opens with Abe, once again, wandering through the

59 'Clyde Fans, Part One, continued', *Palookaville* #12 (May 1998). Note the new styling of the title.

rooms of his apartment, describing his brother's eccentricities and telling the reader something about his own character.

The sense of strange worlds that crops up in 'Clyde Fans' has a believable pretext. These worlds are rooted in Simon's interest in collecting old postcards—novelty freak cards—as Abe calls them, featuring apparently 'giant apples or potatoes ... or pictures of enormous fish being hauled out of a lake.'[60] These photo-collaged images give the sensation that massively over-scaled objects are the norm in the seeming reality of the photographic image. Pondering his brother's curious interest in the freakish world of these pictures, Abe surmises that its source, in retrospect, was 'painfully obvious'. These pictures, constructed by 'oddball entrepreneurs', and 'eccentric hustlers, talented with a camera and a pair of scissors' depict 'little men overwhelmed by huge forces beyond their control.' For Abe, it is an easy leap to see a parallel between Simon and the 'little men' of the pictures. He also offers that the connection was lost on Simon, and in a way the same could be said of Abe who, Seth shows, does not see an analogy between the surrealism of the postcards and the reality he accepts as true.

---

60 *Palookaville* #12.

The tale of the postcards told in 'Clyde Fans' has a whiff of familiarity as a simulacrum of the work that Seth the cartoonist does with his graphic novels, especially 'Clyde Fans' itself. Just as Simon is described as a veritable expert in the arcana of the early part of the twentieth century, so too Seth immerses himself in the forms and conventions of the comics and cartoons of yesteryear. With his depth of knowledge about the personalities and historiography of the form, Seth draws a kind of eccentric collector self-portrait in Simon whose compulsive acquisitiveness echoes Seth's own for the comic art of an earlier generation. In these respects, Simon is a resonant fictional stand-in for Seth in the story of 'Clyde Fans'.

The difference is that Simon's imaginative landscape is cast in the nomenclature of surrealism — banality expressed in radical contrasts. Seth underlines and describes the claustrophobic ordinariness that surrounds Simon. Abe, summarizing their plotless lives in the language of the travelling salesman, says, 'Simon and I, our lives didn't seem to have much of a plot. Perhaps all lives are like that — just a series of events with little meaning. In the end, what kind of pitch was it? Surely Simon failed to close. And myself?'[61]

---

61 *Palookaville* #12.

The difference is that for Seth the artist, the power lay in his talents and imagination to give a plotless and oddly disjunctive narrative cadence, substance, texture, nuance and, ultimately, meaning. 'Clyde Fans' in many respects might be one such attempt to structure an aimless narrative in such a way as to give it moral sententiousness.

A CADENCE OF DISINTEGRATION

The cadence of 'Clyde Fans' is charted in the disintegration of both the family business and Simon's mind; this story is told beginning with *Palookaville* #13, which contains Part 2 of 'Clyde Fans'.[62] Using the trope of a journey through the landscape as a trip in time and into the mind, Seth opens the issue with a marvellously evocative series of panels silently describing a train trip that Simon took in 1957 — a sales trip to Dominion, a town in southern Ontario. Seth deftly portrays a lonely Simon trudging through the empty streets at night in dynamically composed drawings that lead the eye across the page and into the individual compositions from a number of points of view — long shot, aerial shot, close-up and context description.

Grafted onto this 'real-time' narrative, Seth depicts Simon's imaginary conversations with his domineering brother. The curlicue-edged episode panels signify these interactions. Abe looms large in Simon's mind with an imposing, bullying presence. Gradually, as the narrative unfolds with Simon eating in a diner, then meeting a fellow travelling salesman, the reader begins to realize that even the most

---

62 *Palookaville* #13 (July 1999). See pp. 1, 5, and 13, in particular for the variety of points of view Seth uses to describe Simon's trek through the landscape, across the empty street and into the hotel room.

ordinary social activities — a train ride, eating in public — are Simon's everyday terrors. Yet, as Simon admits to himself, the terrors are also opportunities to '*create* an identity for [himself]', perhaps as a salesman, perhaps as something else.[63] That said, Seth quickly disabuses the reader of the notion that Simon's story is anything even close to being a lesson in self-actualization. In his telling of it in *Palookaville* #13 and #14,[64] and in the sombre, noir tones of his drawing style, this is a narrative bathed in wretchedness and infused with loss and depression, so much so that one cannot help but sympathize with Simon who is clearly on the edge of a breakdown. Hounded by a debilitating fear of his overbearing brother, and increasingly anxious in Dominion's downtown crowds, Simon fumbles his way from one unsuccessful sales call to another. Drawing, gesture, composition, style and the interactions of one panel to the next all provide the reader with a nuanced appreciation for Simon's predicament: trapped in a life he does not want to live, completely lacking in self-confidence and wearing an ill-fitting identity that is more a psychic carbuncle than a true expression of who he is as a man.

---

63   *Palookaville* #13 (July 1999).

64   *Palookaville* #14 (2000).

A NOSTALGIC LUDDITE

On the back cover of *Palookaville* #14, Seth published an uncharacteristically long commentary entitled 'Seth Speaks'.[65] In the early days of the twenty-first century, a morose, rebarbative Seth sat down at his typewriter and wrote what amounts to an important admission about why he sees value in the past and emulates mid-twentieth-century styles and expressive modes. Realizing that his affection for the previous century makes him appear as 'some sort of nostalgic luddite', Seth remains unapologetic for his retrieval 'of some of the good things of the past that were lost in the rush to progress.'[66] He writes that the world around him is, to his eyes, becoming increasingly ugly, cheap, and crappy, that the buildings make him feel lousy, and that he is simply not interested in 'most of the cultural slop that is being steered [his] way.' In fact, he seems to suggest that his aversion to most of what contemporary life was producing, in part, convinced him to hold fast — cling — to the designs and values of earlier times,

---

65 'Seth Speaks', *Palookaville* #14, inside back cover.

66 Ibid.

even the fashions. He dressed in the garments of the 1940s and 1950s as a way to get back in touch with a time that seemed simpler and that from the vantage point of a new century was disappearing at a faster and faster pace. Simply and testily, he writes, 'I don't want to be living in the 21st century. I don't even like the sound of it.' As keenly as the loss of time and an era wear on him, Seth also mourns the trashing of the devices of the period — typewriter ribbons, hats, a mailing tube. Above all, he regrets the disappearance of the pulpy paper comic book, a ubiquitous 'common item' of his boyhood growing up in Strathroy and Tilbury in the 1970s and that was such an important part of his artistic and intellectual development.

Seth's uncharacteristic acknowledgement of the reasons he resists change in fashion, style and form can be read as a purposeful declaration of artistic and aesthetic intent. He identifies strongly with the mid-century for many reasons. On the surface, he admires the design motifs, commercial art styles and the way the weekly magazine format, in particular *The New Yorker*, allowed its own visual vocabularies to emerge, not the least of which was the captioned cartoon. Seth embraced its convention of gag line and drawing working together to present a perceptive and humorous truth as a joke. The comic book also fed his developing imagination by inspiring him to invent and draw his own superhero stories.

Above all, and as this diatribe reveals, Seth's sense of connection to this past goes much deeper than surface style. Perhaps projecting a raw sense of the dislocation from what he imagines was a more stable past, he grasps at what he views as an understandable and simple value system. Beauty, courtliness, manners, self-expression, the dignity of manual work, an ability to express and understand nuance, community-mindedness and much more: all these values hold a profound importance to him. They are the elements of a personal identity that gives him a sense of permanence in a world of flux and disruption. These principles are fused onto the imaginary world of Abe and Simon, and are the foundations of his life. In fact, their congruent overlap with the principles infusing *Palookaville* contributes to

the impression of a very thin tissue separating his art from his life. Just as he conjures up in his art a completely integral bucolic vision of southern Ontario more than half a century gone, so he lives it out—performs it—in the way he conducts his life away from the drawing board. Nostalgic luddite may be an overly hard self-characterization, but nevertheless there is clearly contentment in the idea of a pre-digital utopia. *Palookaville* is many things, but it is also a kind of urgent, postmodern *samizdat* wherein Seth can voice his cleverly disguised dystopian warnings about the consequences of depending too much on the machinery of a digital society. A luddite of a different sort: a prophet warning of decline wrought by digital technology.

A TRAGIC ANTIHERO

Through the character of Simon, Seth also describes the dire fate of a soul dramatically removed from his path of self-actualization. As Seth charts Simon's breakdown, he creates a truly remarkable artistic interpretation of psychosis. Simon's disintegration is not expressed gratuitously or in a voice of judgement and ridicule; it is sensitively portrayed in the subtle blurring of reality with delusion that infects Simon's mind with strange, uncanny personifications

and projections. Propelled by the opprobrium of brutish Abe, Simon is shown becoming so unnerved by his lack of success that failure becomes a self-fulfilling prophecy. He believes so deeply that he will never be capable of making a sale that he falls apart professionally and personally.

Seth brilliantly charts this tragic unwinding through issues #15 and #16.[67] Using very little dialogue, Seth allows his drawing to give 'voice' to the destructive vortex that overwhelms Simon. He also compresses reality and memory to such an extent that the present in which Simon stumbles around resonates with confusing images from the past, and from the depths of his consciousness. The blurring is so convincing that Seth seamlessly transforms Simon's lonely world into a veritable metaphor of his damaged soul. Toys speak to him, chide and rebuke him, and he argues back at them. Abe's haunting presence looms large in his mind, clouding his perception of events. A recollection about a lighthouse turns hallucinatory, dreamlike, causing visions to emanate in front of him, and making the rational become bizarre.

Seth displays an unusually refined talent for giving peculiarity a sympathetic cast. Simon's irrational reality is set down, paradoxically, in a clearly drawn dream play. The panels and pages exhibit an innate structure that amplifies the cinematic scope of the narrative described in a drawn work in the noir genre. His are masterful interpretations of ambiguity, delusion, waning sanity and tragic fatalism without a trace of cynicism. The artist carefully, lovingly renders Simon, the antihero, losing touch. Never cast as a loser, Simon is more the innocent victim of society's indifference, Abe's malevolence and paranoia. Compelling, beautiful graphic storytelling of a very high order is in evidence in Seth's silent, wordless sequences showing

---

67   *Palookaville* #15 (May 2001); *Palookaville* #16 (2002).

Simon stumbling through a rocky wasteland to a lighthouse, then ascending its spiral staircase and gazing through a window into the turret's centre; in his aerial rendering of Dominion's inhuman downtown core; in the nightmarish depiction of a miniature-golf park; and in his charting of Simon's climb to 'a sort of enchanted place' at the end of the second part of the story.

'A SORT OF FOOTPRINT'

Although the cartoons are witness to a sad story, they also serve to reveal a grand theme occupying 'Clyde Fans' — one that could also be considered as testifying to an important part of Seth's aesthetic and world view: What constitutes a true portrait? *Palookaville* #16 shows Seth exploring various narrative voices to tell his story from multiple viewpoints. He uses silence and wordlessness to great effect, letting his drawings alone open up interior monologues. He has Simon speak of himself in the third person as well as the first to give the reader a sense of detachment and intimacy. And he flashes back and forth in historical time to provide both context and motivation for character development.

But it is in Simon's interior monologue, set down in a cursive script reminiscent of a journal entry, that much is revealed about both Simon and Seth. Seth's panels showing Simon ambling through the apartment in 1966 take on the aura of a philosophical inquiry on the shape of time and the location of memory. Simon's musings on the magical powers of incantation to conjure up places and people from his past have a kind of self-reference about them to the extent that it is not too much of a leap to read on these pages Seth himself meditating on the very nature of *his* artistic project unfolding in the pages of *Palookaville*. Through Simon, Seth asks the simple yet profound questions that, as he says, leave 'a sort of footprint' on a person that remains as time passes by. 'That footprint is still there. There is an odd connecting thread between you and that solitary creature.'[68]

In essence, through the character and voice of Simon, Seth takes the reader into a contemplative passage on the idea of *dasein*, the German word for a philosophic concept examined by Martin Heidegger — of being in the moment, and equally aware that it is impossible to be in the moment. Time moves on. In what may well be one of the more tragically poignant remarks in all the *Palookaville* episodes, Simon observes of his beloved treasure box containing his favourite collection of objects that, 'Sometimes, I imagine that if I could just remember these objects [in my treasure box], find them again, and place them back in the box in just the right order, then (like a magic recipe) it would open up that time barrier and I'd be on the other side … in a better moment.'[69] Truth be told, *Palookaville* is that treasure box. It functions for Seth, and perhaps for the reader, in the way Simon wants his box to function.

---

68 *Palookaville* #16.

69 Ibid.

PORTRAIT OF PSYCHOSIS

On *Palookaville* #16's back cover, Seth has placed an ad for back issues of 'Clyde Fans'. He describes it in the tagline: 'A middle-aged man (filled with dread) walks about silently for 70 or more pages. The excitement knows no bounds.'[70] But there is drama of a much different and riveting sort in the development of Simon's character. In drawing Simon, Seth has crafted a richly complex portrait of a man in deep distress, losing his grip on reality, suffering from some form of delusional psychosis. Simon is a tragic, self-loathing figure absolutely isolated from the world around him. Seth has drawn a meditation on the passage of moments, the passage of individual identities, which in aggregate define a life as it ages. Simon muses on his past: 'Was that an earlier Simon? Perhaps as each successive Simon has come along, the meaning has grown weaker … like a mirror reflecting a mirror, reflecting a mirror.'[71] In a dream sequence in which Simon sees himself drowning, Seth beautifully emblematizes the emotional trouble that might literally be killing him. Further along in panels depicting one of Simon's interior monologues, he comes to an important

70 'Palookaville Department Store', back cover of *Palookaville* #16.

71 *Palookaville* #17 (July 2004).

self-analysis. As he continues to wander through the darkened apartment, he makes this admission and observation:

This brings me to an interesting topic — something I just recently came to understand. You see, after years of viewing this place [the apartment] as a prison, I suddenly saw that it and I were the same thing. You'll likely see this as a kind of metaphor but I don't mean it that way. I'm speaking literally. This building is an appendage of mine like an arm or a neck. It's a shell that I secreted to protect my weak, crumbling and cluttered interior. That shell may have a hard physicality to it, but it's here, in this pulpy centre, where reality is at its most solid. Outside the shell — it's all illusion. Trust me, as horrid as it is in here — it's worse out there …[72]

Metaphor or not, through Simon Seth points to an important symbiotic relationship between the brothers and the apartment, and he also deploys the uncanny magic of a graphic novel to add nuance to the inner and outer realities that define a whole character. Abe's and Simon's inner landscapes are mirrored in the present-day empty, decaying shell of rooms. Moments of self-awareness, of peeling back

---

72 *Palookaville* #17 (July 2004).

the onionskins of past lives and memories, are finely revealed in the trudgings in and out of the warrens of the apartment. The aimless meanderings mirror the fumbling attempts to come to grips with failure and loneliness, and to find in whatever is left of a crumbling home some shards of a dissolving identity. In this, Seth has created a disturbing picture of Palookaville in which Abe and Simon seemed trapped, unable to escape. Theirs is definitely a one-way ticket, no matter how hard they both try to resurface into lives of health and happiness. They are doomed to perdition.

TURNING INTO A BIRD

An antihero, a tragic figure, a man losing his mind, Simon is all of these wrapped in whole cloth as a hapless misfit. 'Clyde Fans, part three, continued', published in *Palookaville* #18, is one of the finest, most sensitive interpretations of a man losing his grip by sliding into psychosis.[73] It begins with Seth drawing attention to the tiny event of Simon observing sun and shadow on his hands and on the papers of his desk. This moment crystallizes the fact in Simon's mind that he is getting old — that time is moving forward — even though he (Simon

---

73 *Palookaville* #18 (October 2005).

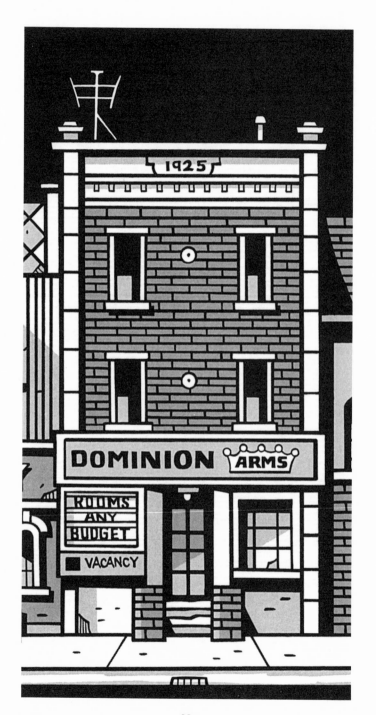

and Seth) has been trying to hold it back in an unconscious way. In subsequent panels, Seth revisits the conceit of using his strip as a way to meditate on a larger issue through the actions of his characters. In this instance, Simon, contemplating his postcard-collecting hobby, observes that the hobby is his attempt to halt time by 'remarkably reordering reality.'[74] His cards, he comes to realize, hint at another time and another place. This thought process leads Simon to proceed to thinking about death as an event that finally stops the 'forward movement of time for good'. The incessant momentum of time plodding along in a fateful inevitability: these realities lead Simon to distraction and the realization that, 'You can't fix yourself in time no matter how hard you try.'

As self-evident as this statement is, it signifies a profound moment not only in Simon's life, but also in 'Clyde Fans'—and perhaps even in *Palookaville* itself. If the project is a means for the author to explore a microscopically thin separation between art and life, between fiction and autobiography, and the innate pathos in any effort to stop time, even by means of art, then Simon's prescient statement could stand as the moral of the story and of *Palookaville*. Time cannot stand still in real life, but the uncanny magic of this cartoon graphic novel is that the author has the creative power to toy with time's shape, trajectory and velocity. As Simon over the edge, Seth masterfully represents his breakdown in a series of surreal panels showing him transforming into a fedora-wearing bird.

But what is the true cause of Simon's collapse? It is a product of his fraught relationship with his brother. It has something to do with his unrealized potential and his interest as a collector of arcana and surreal postcards. The fact that he failed to examine his unique interests as important elements in his healthy self-identity contributed to

---

74   *Palookaville* #18 (October 2005).

a feeling of alienation and a lingering sense of incompleteness. Anxiety over the passing of time, fear of a predetermined fate that was malevolent, emptiness left by the absence of a father, sadness at the knowledge that his has been an unexamined life, and the keenly felt identification with a past era, these and other factors all contributed to Simon's malaise. But the most debilitating of all the factors that put Simon over the edge might well be traced in the *Palookaville* series to the crippling effects of the abiding sadness he felt in his mother's apparent dementia. The arc of 'Clyde Fans' can be traced in the story of Simon coming to the realization that his mother has an illness that has robbed her of her mind, and has taken her from him. Loss and longing: these are the big themes of the graphic novel that Seth interprets in the complex, multi-layered narrative 'Clyde Fans'.

As complex as the narrative lines are, the graphic storytelling methods Seth uses also show an artist fearlessly exploring the visual vocabularies of cartoons and comic books. In reading *Palookaville*, what is revealed is an artist coming into his own as a graphic designer, draughtsman and as someone who has developed a unique fluency in the method of drawing an epic tale, and of making fully his own a wide spectrum of ways in which a visual story can be laid out and designed on a page. *Palookaville* #19, particularly on page 74, is an object lesson on how a holistic contextual landscape can be at the same time a foundational structure for episodic panels. Seth beautifully describes Simon traipsing through a squalid, dilapidated back

alley and coming to the realization that he has seen this place before. This sequence is graphic novel writing and drawing of a very high order.[75]

A NEW FORMAT

Palookaville continues. The comic has morphed into a new iteration as a small format, hard-covered booklet containing the continuing saga of Clyde Fans' declining fortunes and transformation into Borealis Business Machines.[76] Without new stock and replacement parts supplied by Borealis, Clyde Fans runs down and goes belly up. Throughout all the sad changes in the company, plus broken marriages and labour troubles, Abe and Simon manage to continue their awkward fraternal relationship. Time marches on despite attempts to arrest it in the conventions of graphic autobiography and in the fictional world of the Matchcard brothers.

Palookaville's changed format, which carries on through issue #22, gives Seth the range to add different departments to his publication. Inasmuch as one of the overriding themes of the graphic novel is

75 *Palookaville* #19 (February 2008).

76 'Welcome to the new Palookaville', *Palookaville* #20 (2010).

the shape of time, its inevitable, incessant, fateful march, and the merits and consequences of resisting change, the comic book itself ironically transforms. In addition to the continuing saga of 'Clyde Fans' it includes chapters on Seth's sculptural project 'Dominion City',[77] selections from his sketchbooks,[78] his rubber-stamping process,[79] photographic essays[80] and the plaintive episodic narrative 'Nothing Lasts' (perhaps even more autobiographical than 'Clyde Fans').[81]

Despite the embedded mistrust of change that fuels *Palookaville*'s stories, this graphic episodic novel, disguised as a comic book, is an emblem of creative inquiry and a testament to remarkable artistic agility. It is built on a rich and deep tradition of cartooning that reached an apogee in the mid-century in Canada and the United States, a period close to Seth's heart and that is the foundation of his personal and artistic identities. It builds upon its artistic antecedents in a way that is wholly contemporary. Stylistically Seth absorbs and reinterprets the genre's vocabularies and iconographies in an apparently boundless way to create characters and stories of complexity, nuance and abiding humanity.

By working in the manner of his artistic soulmates, in *Palookaville*

---

77   Ibid., pp. 31–59.

78   'Selections from sketchbooks seven & eight', *Palookaville* #20, beginning on p. 60, and following to end of issue.

79   'Rubber stamp diary', *Palookaville* #21 (September 2013), beginning on p.65 and following.

80   'Crown Barber', *Palookaville* #22 (April 2015).

81   'Nothing Lasts', Part One (from sketchbook # 10), *Palookaville* #21; 'Nothing Lasts', Part Two, *Palookaville* #22.

Seth redefines the forms and conventions of the comic book and the cartoon. But more than that, in transforming an artistic form, he has created a magnificently complete reality defined by the baleful lives and times of his characters. His project is prosaic, superbly drawn, imaginatively conceived and deftly executed. It exposes the tragic consequences of lives lived in ways that are inauthentic through graphic novellas about the vicious beating of an ambiguously gendered young man, and about an adulterous fling. The search for Kalo traces a fruitless search for a man who perhaps failed to embrace his fate with open arms. Simon and Abe's failures are exposed in their fear of defining themselves by engaging with the times in which they lived. Try as they might, they cannot stop time. Rather than live in the moment, they hold fast to a myth of the past that is rapidly dissolving. Abandonment, loss, disappointment, despair, anxiety, anger and neuroses: Seth's *Palookaville* explores a terminal point on a one-way ticket down.

Yet Seth redeems the characters and places he draws by his own example and manner. In telling their stories, and in 'performing' them as elements of his own biography, Seth shows how art can elevate and make sense of lives and times, and of the complex proposition of just *being* a human being.

ACKNOWLEDGEMENTS

My thanks to the many people who provided me with assistance as I researched and wrote this article. In particular, I am grateful to Seth, who patiently answered my many questions. I would also like to express my appreciation to the team at the Porcupine's Quill: Tim and Elke Inkster, Don McLeod, Stephanie Small, and particularly, Chandra Wohleber; my colleagues at the Peel Art Gallery, Museum and Archives: Marty Brent, Annemarie Hagan, Angie Warner, Gerrie Loveys, Sonja Hidas and Rachel Leaton. They all came together to bring this project to life. The Ontario Arts Council gave valuable financial support along the way. — *Tom Smart*